1

one

un

2

two

deux

3

three

Trois

4

four

quatre

5

five

cinq

6

six

six

7

seven

Sept

8

eight

huit

9

nine

neuf

10

ten

Dix

11

eleven

Onze

12

twelve

Douze

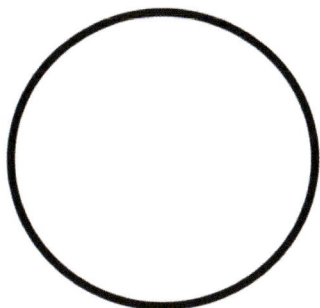

white

blanche

black

noir

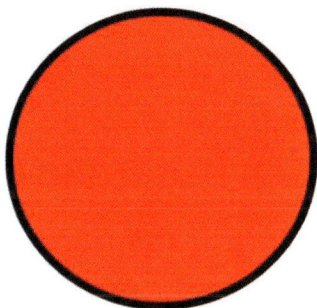

red

rouge

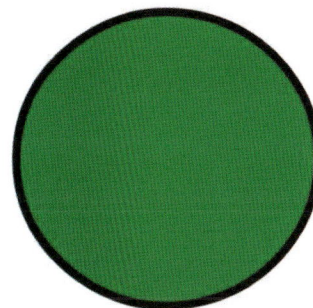

green

vert

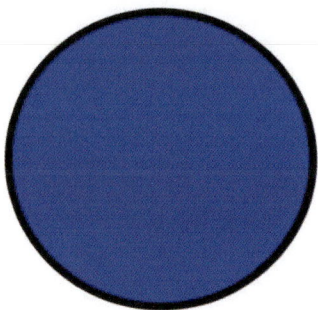

blue

bleu

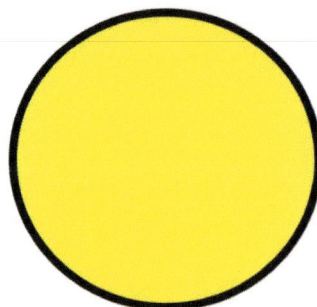

yellow

jaune

crimson

cramoisi

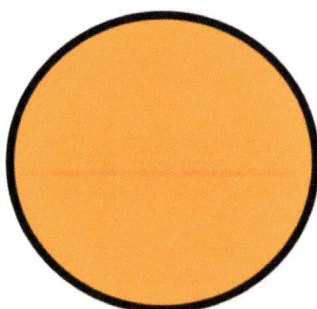

orange

Orange

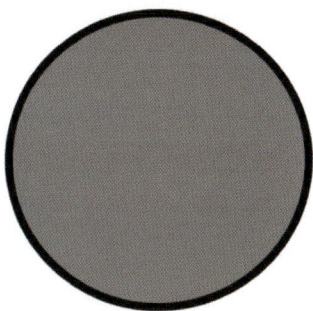

gray

gris

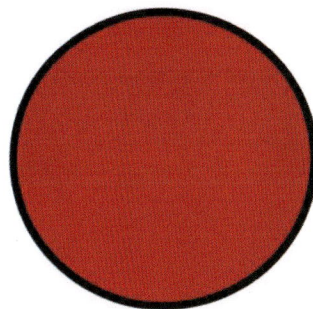

brown

brun

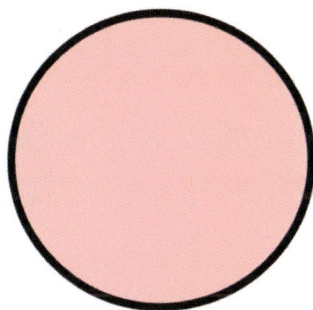

pink

rose

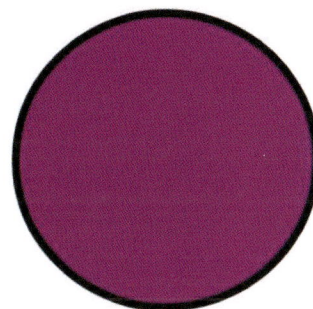

purple

violet

grandpa

grand-père

grandma

grand-mère

father

père

mother

mère

brother

frère

sister

sœur

son

fils

daughter

fille

apple

Pomme

banana

banane

orange

Orange

lemon

citron

avocado

avocat

strawberry

fraise

watermelon

pastèque

grape

raisin

pomegranate

Grenade

pineapple

ananas

kiwi

kiwi

mango

mangue

potato

Patate

carrot

carotte

onion

oignon

cabbage

choux

Tomatoes

Tomates

Cucumber

Concombre

Lettuce

laitue

Peas

Pois

foot

pied

eye

œil

ear

oreille

mouth

bouche

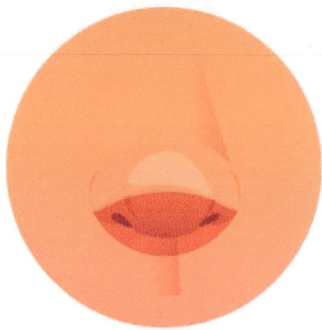

nose

nez

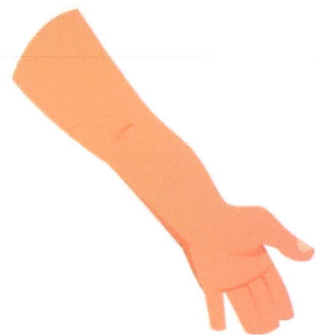

arm

bras

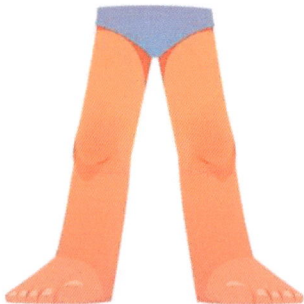

leg

jambe

hand

main

dog

chien

cat

chat

fish

poisson

horse

cheval

chicken

poulet

sheep

mouton

frog

grenouille

rabbit

lapin

monkey

singe

Pig

Cochon

cow

vache

goat

chèvre

doctor

médecin

chef

chef

fireman

pompier

farms

fermier

Architect

Architecte

Policeman

Policier

nurse

infirmière

Lawyer

Avocat

car

voiture

taxi

Taxi

fire truck

camion de pompier

ambulance

ambulance

police car

voiture de police

bus

autobus

Train

train

airplane

avion

socks

chaussettes

shoes

chaussures

t-shirt

T-shirt

hat

chapeau

Trousers

Pantalon

dress

robe

jacket

veste

Sunglasses

lunettes de soleil

winter

hiver

summer

été

spring

printemps

autumn

automne

Printed in Great Britain
by Amazon